T. H. James

The Matsuyama Mirror

T. H. James

The Matsuyama Mirror

ISBN/EAN: 9783744704182

Printed in Europe, USA, Canada, Australia, Japan

Cover: Foto ©Thomas Meinert / pixelio.de

More available books at **www.hansebooks.com**

Japanese Fairy Tale Series. No. 10.

THE MATSUYAMA MIRROR.

Told to
Children
by
Mrs. T. H. James.

Published by the

日本昔噺第十號

松山鏡

英國デイムス夫人編述　定價金拾貳錢

日本　鮮齋永濯画

明治十九年十一月一日版權免許

同　十二月　出版

出版人　東京府平民　長谷川武次郎

出版所　東京府京橋區弥左衛門町二番地　弘文社

THE
MATSUYAMA
MIRROR.

A long long time ago, there lived in a quiet spot, a young man and his wife. They had one child, a little daughter, whom they both loved with all their hearts. I cannot tell you their names, for they have been long since forgotten, but the name of the place where they lived was Matsuyama, in the province of Echigo.

It happened once, while the little girl was still a baby, that the father was obliged to go to the great city, the capital of Japan, upon some business. It was too far for the mother and her little baby to go, so he set out alone, after bidding them good bye, and promising to bring them home some pretty present.

The mother had never been further from home than the next village, and she could not help being a little frightened at the thought of her husband taking

such a long journey, and yet she was a little proud too, for he was the first man in all that country side who had been to the big town where the King and his great lords lived, and where there were so many beautiful and curious things to be seen.

At last the time came when she might expect her husband back, so she dressed the baby in its best clothes, and herself put on a pretty blue dress which she knew her husband liked.

You may fancy how glad this

good wife was to see him come
home safe and sound, and how
the little girl clapped her hands,
and laughed with delight, when

she saw the pretty toys her father had brought for her. He had much to tell of all the wonderful things he had seen upon the journey, and in the town itself.

"I have brought you a very pretty thing," said he to his wife: "it is called a mirror. Look and tell me what you see inside." He gave to her plain, white wooden box, in which, when she had opened it, she found a round piece of metal. One side was white like frosted silver, and ornamented with raised figures of birds and flowers, the other was bright as

the clearest crystal. Into it the
young mother looked with delight
and astonishment, for, from its
depths was looking at her with
parted lips and bright eyes, a
smiling happy face.

"What do you see?" again asked the husband, pleased at her astonishment, and glad to show that he had learned something while he had been away. "I see a pretty woman looking at me, and she moves her lips as if she was speaking, and—dear me, how odd, she has on a blue dress just like mine!" "Why, you silly woman, it is your own face that you see," said the husband, proud of knowing something that his wife didn't know. That round piece of metal is called a mirror, in the town every body has one, although we have not seen them in this country place before.

The wife was charmed with her present, and, for a few days could not look into the mirror often enough, for you must remember, that, as this was the first time she had seen a mirror, so, of course, it was the first time she had ever seen the reflection of her own pretty face. But she considered such a wonderful thing far too precious for every day use, and soon shut it up in its box again, and put it away carefully among her most valued treasures.

Years past on, and the husband and wife still lived happily. The joy of their life was their little daughter, who grew up the very image of her mother, and who was so dutiful and affectionate that every body loved her. Mindful of her own little passing vanity on finding herself so lovely, the mother kept the mirror carefully hidden away, fearing that the use of it might breed a spirit of pride in her little girl.

She never spoke of it, and as for the father, he had forgotten all about it. So it happened that the daughter grew up as simple as the mother had been, and knew nothing of her own good looks, or of the mirror which would have reflectd them.

But bye and bye a terrible misfortune happened to this happy little family. The good, kind mother fell sick; and, although her daughter waited upon her day and night, with loving care, she got worse and worse, until at last there was no hope but that she must die.

When she found that she must so soon leave her husband and child, the poor woman felt very sorrowful, grieving for those she was going to leave behind, and most of all for her little daughter.

She called the girl to her and said; "My darling child, you know that I am very sick: soon I must die, and and leave your dear father and you alone. When I am gone, promise me that you will look into this mirror every night and every morning: there you will see me, and know that I am still watching over you." With these words she took the mirror from its hiding place and gave it to her daughter. The child promised,

with many tears, and so the mother, seeming now calm and resigned, died a short time after.

Now this obedient and dutiful daughter, never forgot her mother's last request, but each morning and evening took the mirror from its hiding place, and looked in it long and earnestly. There she saw the bright and smiling vision of her lost mother. Not pale and sickly as in her last days, but the beautiful young mother of long ago. To her at night she told the story of the trials and difficulties of the day, to her in the morning she looked for sympathy and encouragement in whatever might be in store for her.

So day by day she lived as in her mother's sight, striving still to please her as she had done in her life time, and careful always to avoid whatever might pain or grieve her.

Her greatest joy was to be able to look in the mirror and say; "Mother, I have been today what you would have me to be."

Seeing her every night and morning, without fail, look into the mirror, and seem to hold converse with it, her father at length asked her the reason of her strange behaviour. "Father," she said, "I look in the mirror every day to see my dear mother and to talk with her." Then she told him of her mother's dying wish, and how she had never failed to fulfil it. Touched by so much simplicity, and such faithful, loving obedience, the father

shed tears of pity and affection. Nor could he find it in his heart to tell the child, that the image she saw in the mirror, was but the reflection of her own sweet face, by constant

sympathy and association, becoming more and more like her dead mother's day by day.